Wearable Robots

by Carla Mooney

NORWOODHOUSE PRESS

Cover: This wearable robot was designed by the Raytheon Corporation.

Norwood House Press
P.O. Box 316598
Chicago, Illinois 60631

For information regarding Norwood House Press, please visit our website at:
www.norwoodhousepress.com or call 866-565-2900.

Paperback ISBN: 978-1-60357-868-4

The Library of Congress has cataloged the original hardcover edition with the following call number: 2015032148

297R—092016
Printed in ShenZhen, Guangdong, China.

CONTENTS

Note: Words that are **bolded** in the text are defined in the glossary.

CHAPTER 1

Overcoming the Limits of the Human Body

At the 2014 FIFA World Cup Brazil, 29-year-old Juliano Pinto walked onto the grassy field. The crowd was amazed as he kicked a soccer ball to officially open the tournament. What made this moment so amazing is that Pinto is paralyzed from the waist down. In order to kick the ball, he was assisted by a wearable robotic suit.

The suit let Pinto move his legs just by thinking about it. The cap he wore on his head had robotic **sensors**. These sensors picked up his brain signals. They sent the signals to a computer that he carried in a backpack. First the computer **decoded** the brain signals, then it sent a message to the robotic suit's legs and told them how to move. The suit responded and moved Pinto's legs. As the world watched, the paralyzed man kicked the soccer ball.

What Is a Robotic Exoskeleton?

On TV and in the movies, people with superhuman strength do incredible feats. They lift impossible weights. They run extremely fast. They can even jump to super heights. Wearable robots may one day bring the movies to life. They may make regular people stronger and faster than ever.

A robotic **exoskeleton** is a wearable robot. It has joints and limbs that

Juliano Pinto, assisted by a robotic suit at the 2014 FIFA World Cup Brazil.

match the human body. It is a mobile machine that senses and anticipates the wearer's movements. A system of **hydraulic** motors powers it. The suit's motors provide the energy to move the suit's limbs. With the suit, the wearer needs to use less energy.

The Need for Robotic Exoskeletons

The human body is a very complex machine, yet there are limits on what it can do. No matter how much a person trains, he or she will only be able to lift so much weight. The body can only run so fast or

A robotic exoskeleton is worn by a person and has joints and limbs run by hydraulics which provide the energy.

jump so high. Unfortunately, straining or overextending a body's limits can result in injury or paralysis. When this happens, there are limits to how much it can recover. Sometimes a paralyzed patient can never move his or her limbs again.

The search for ways to improve the performance of the human body started in the 1960s. In 1963 US Army researcher Serge Zaroodny designed the first wearable robot. His robot would give its wearer super strength. Unfortunately, his design was just an idea on paper. At the time, the technology to create such a wearable robot did not exist.

Early Attempts

In the mid-1960s many scientists tried to build a robotic exoskeleton. Engineer

DID YOU KNOW?

In the 1800s Edward S. Ellis's science fiction novel *The Steam Man of the Prairies* introduced the idea of a mechanical man.

Neil Mizen from Cornell University was one of them. He researched a wearable exoskeleton. His suit was nicknamed the "superman suit" or the "man **amplifier**." He designed the suit with powered gears at the joints. These gears would give the wearer extra support and strength. He hoped the suit would let a wearer lift 1,000 pounds (454kg) in each hand. Unfortunately, the powered gear system

Iron Man

In 1963 Marvel Comics introduced a new character. He was called Iron Man. In the comic, engineer Tony Stark suffers a severe chest injury and makes a powered suit to save his life. The suit gives him superhuman strength and **durability**. It enables him to fly and equips him with many weapons. Stark dons the suit to protect the world as the superhero Iron Man. The Iron Man character may have inspired many engineers to build a robotic exoskeleton.

In 1963 Marvel Comics introduced Iron Man. He used an exoskeleton suit that gave him superhuman strength and abilities.

The Hardiman suit was developed by General Electric and the US military, however, it too had its flaws.

had flaws, and the man amplifier was never completed.

In 1965 General Electric and the US military worked together to develop the Hardiman suit. Using Mizen's previous research and expanding their resources, they designed a suit that would let its wearer lift 1,500 pounds (680kg). When they built their suit, they too ran into many problems. The suit was too heavy to be worn and it was also very hard to control.

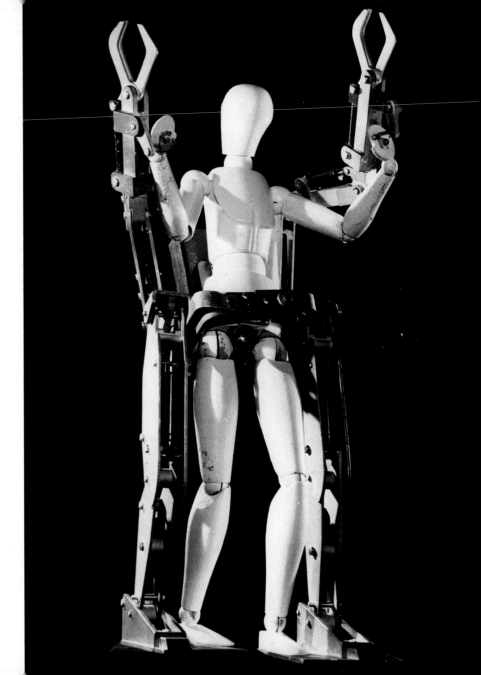

? DID YOU KNOW?

When designing the man amplifier, researchers used photos of a model's movements while wearing a mock-up of the device.

Because of these problems, the project was left unfinished.

For thirty years, the idea of a suit that could improve human strength and endurance remained just a dream. Then, in 1997 the Japanese research firm Cyberdyne made a **prototype** of the Hybrid Assistive Limb (HAL). This HAL prototype was built at the University of Tsukuba. Experts hoped it would help disabled and elderly people with daily activities. Much like previous attempts, this prototype was flawed and hard to use. Because it was constantly attached to a computer it was also heavy to wear. Its batteries alone weighed 49 pounds (22kg).

While many early attempts to build a robotic exoskeleton failed, researchers kept working on designs. For many years scientists were limited by technology. Computers were too slow and not powerful enough for the complex processing needed to make the exoskeletons work right. Scientists had not found a good portable source of energy to power the suits. Many parts of the suits were too weak and bulky to work right. In spite of these challenges, scientists kept researching new ways to build a working wearable robot.

Employees of Cyberdyne, Inc. cross a street wearing the Hybrid Assisted Limb (HAL).

Technology Advances

By 2000 much of the technology that had limited wearable robots in the past had improved. Computers were faster and had more power. Sensors were smaller and easier to use. Some people thought that the time was right to try building a new wearable robot.

In 2000 the Defense Advanced Research Projects Agency (DARPA) launched a seven-year, $75 million program called Exoskeletons for Human Performance Augmentation. Its goal was to build a wearable robot for soldiers. DARPA's wish list for the robot was long. It wanted the wearable

The Pitman Suit

In the 1980s Jeffrey Moore was an engineer at the Los Alamos National Lab. He designed a robotic suit to give its wearer super strength. Named the Pitman suit, it was supposed to be a powered suit of armor for soldiers. Moore proposed to control the exoskeleton with a network of brain-scanning sensors. These would be in a helmet. He said that the sensors would measure the shift in magnetic fields when the brain sent messages to move the body. The Defense Department doubted Moore could make his idea work, and therefore turned him down.

robot to help soldiers carry hundreds of pounds and hike for days without getting tired. Soldiers wearing this robot would be able to handle weapons that usually required two people. They could lift and carry injured soldiers off the battlefield. The robotic suit would let soldiers wear more protective armor. Soldiers wearing it could even jump higher.

Many experts did not think that DARPA's idea for a wearable robot was realistic. They thought it was impossible to build such a suit. DARPA researchers set out to prove them wrong.

DID YOU KNOW?

One of the first robotic exoskeletons was designed by Nicholas Yagn of Russia in 1890.

CHAPTER 2

Real-Life Iron Man: Making It Move

The robotic exoskeleton that DARPA wanted proved to be a huge challenge. To be usable, it would have to be powerful and easy to use safely. Together, these elements needed to be combined into a functional device.

To work, the exoskeleton would have to read a soldier's motions and copy them instantly. If a soldier swung his left arm, the exoskeleton would have to swing at the same time. It would also have to swing in the same direction and with the right amount of force. If it was too slow, it would drag on the limb. The wearer would feel as if he or she were trying to move through water. The suit would also need to read the forces applied across the suit. It would need to have powerful **microprocessors** to translate that data into instructions for the robot's limbs.

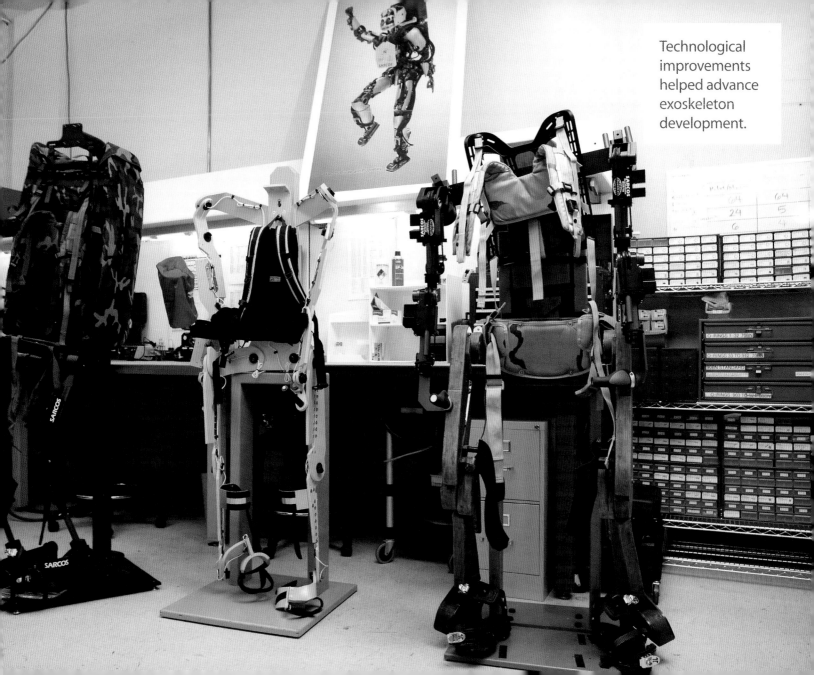

Technological improvements helped advance exoskeleton development.

To solve this problem, DARPA turned to Steve Jacobsen. He was the founder of a bioengineering research company called Sarcos. He had built robotic dinosaurs, **prosthetics**, and human-computer interfaces. He was also skilled in software and mechanical engineering and had a talent for inventing what he needed. If a part did not exist, he would design his own. His skill and creativity made him ideal to take on the exoskeleton challenge.

Designing an Interface

One of the biggest problems facing the exoskeleton was its interface. An interface is a connection between two things. How would the robot connect and respond to the human wearing it? Jacobsen thought that he had a way to do this.

To test his idea, he asked Jon Price, Sarcos's staff photographer, and Price's daughter to join him in an experiment.

BLEEX

Researchers at the University of California–Berkeley also worked to design an exoskeleton for the DARPA program. They came up with the Berkeley Lower Extremity Exoskeleton (BLEEX). It was first made in 2004. The prototype let wearers carry up to 200 pounds (91kg) on their backs and not feel extra weight. The BLEEX was also able to move over rough **terrain** for long periods of time. If the device lost power, the wearer could remove its legs and turn it into a standard backpack.

In the test, Price acted as the exoskeleton, while his daughter played the operator. She stood on her dad's feet, with her toes on top of his. Her back faced her dad. The pair held hands for balance. Then the girl began to walk. Price tried to stay in step with her and keep his feet directly below hers. In a few minutes, the pair moved in sync. The girl decided how fast to walk and when to turn and Price copied her with each step. Their success proved to Jacobsen that his idea would work. With a few points of contact, a smart machine could interpret the movements of a person strapped to it. Then it could react in the right way.

Jacobsen and his team began to create an exoskeleton. He strapped his first test suit on an engineer in 2002. The engineer tried out different movements. These tests helped Jacobsen figure out the right range of motion and the right places for joints. In 2003 the team began to work on getting the joints to open and close with the right speed and power. Sarcos decided to use hydraulic **actuators** as mechanical muscles. He also designed sensors that could detect the user's muscle contractions. The sensors operated valves that controlled the flow of high-pressure hydraulic fluid to the robot's joints. The joints moved cylinders with cables. These acted like **tendons** attached to human muscles.

Raytheon Sarcos XOS Prototype

In 2007 the Raytheon Company bought Sarcos. It continued Jacobsen's work.

Steve Jacobsen (right) helped build the Raytheon Sarcos XOS (left).

In 2008 the company built the Raytheon Sarcos XOS. The exoskeleton works like a human limb. When a person curls an arm, muscle fibers in the upper arm contract. This pulls tendons that lift the forearm. In the XOS a sensor in the handle detects a force when the wearer moves an arm. The sensor sends the data to a computer and control system that is located on the back of the suit. The computer detects the force and direction needed to move the XOS. It sends instructions to valves that control the flow of hydraulic fluid to cylinder actuators in the suit's joints. When the fluid moves the cylinders, they move cables attached to the cylinders. Acting like a tendon, this pulls on the suit's arm.

The XOS has sensors in the hand grips and in the suit's feet and back. The computer uses this data to figure out the position and motion of the suit's arms, legs, and back. It can tell how the wearer wants to move. Then it figures out what the suit needs to do to mirror that movement. When wearing the XOS, the user never feels strain. The XOS system tells its robotic arms to grab the weight before the user exerts any significant force.

Improving the Design

In 2010 Raytheon Sarcos built the XOS 2. This version was lighter, stronger, and faster than the XOS. At the same time, it used 50 percent less power. A person wearing the XOS 2 can lift about 200 pounds (91kg) of weight for long periods of time and not feel strain. Wearers can also punch through 3 inches (7.6cm) of wood. A soldier wearing the XOS 2 can do the work of three soldiers.

DID YOU KNOW?

The XOS has 30 actuators. Each controls a different joint on the exoskeleton.

Gait Rehabilitation

When people have a stroke, brain injury, or spinal cord injury, they may lose their ability to walk. Fortunately, the human brain can relearn things. With training and therapy, some patients can relearn how to walk. This process is called **gait rehabilitation**. Some hospitals and therapy centers use robotic exoskeletons to help people with gait rehabilitation.

A patient undergoes gait rehabilitation to relearn how to walk.

Sensors in the hands, feet and back provide computer data that tells the suit how to react.

The XOS 2 is attached to an internal combustion hydraulics engine by a wire. This engine is the suit's power source. It drives the suit's hydraulic actuators. Sensors in the suit send information about the position and force needed to move its limbs. On the XOS 2, computer processors are located at every joint on the suit. The sensors send signals to these processors. The signals prompt the actuators to deliver about

440 pounds (199 kilograms) of force per square centimeter. A person wearing the suit can lift large amounts of weight over and over again and not feel strain.

There are some limits to the XOS 2 exoskeleton. The largest limitation is that the suit is not self-powered. It is attached to a **stationary** power source. To solve this problem, Raytheon Sarcos is working on a backpack power source that could provide power for at least eight hours. Eventually, it hopes to make the suit self-powered.

In a short time, robotic exoskeletons like the XOS 2 promise to help the human body do more than ever before possible. They are ready to make a difference in people's lives worldwide.

CHAPTER 3

Robotic Exoskeletons at Work

Robotic exoskeletons may one day make life easier for thousands of people. Exoskeletons can improve the lives of soldiers by offering aided assistance when wearing heavy protective gear. They may ease the strain on factory workers. They may even help paralyzed patients walk. One person whose life will be impacted is Daniel Fukuchi. He is partly paralyzed from the waist down.

Helping People Walk

In 1999 Fukuchi was an active teenager. He enjoyed rollerblading and riding bikes. In August 1999 Fukuchi went on vacation in Hawaii before beginning his first year of college. One morning, he went surfing. While there, he felt a throbbing pain in his lower back. He thought it was a muscle strain and ignored it. Soon he also noticed that his legs felt weak. He returned to his hotel to rest. Over the next few hours, his symptoms got worse. By the time he went to the hospital, Fukuchi was completely paralyzed from the waist down.

Doctors told Fukuchi he had transverse myelitis. This is a rare disorder. It is caused by swelling in the spinal cord. Over the next seven years, Fukuchi slowly got back some feeling and motion in his legs, but he still needed a wheelchair and crutches to move. Then he heard about a test program at the Berkeley Robotics & Human Engineering Lab. It was run by robotics expert Homayoon Kazerooni. Kazerooni was working on exoskeletons to help people with disabilities and he was looking for people to test his exoskeleton.

Fukuchi contacted Kazerooni and became part of the test program. Each week, Fukuchi visits Kazerooni's lab and tests the exoskeleton. The device straps to his waist and thighs. It is powered by two motors at the hips that move his legs forward. To take a step, he pushes a button on a handheld controller. The exoskeleton helps him walk farther and faster than he can on crutches. He says that using it helps him maintain his strength and balance. He thinks that the exoskeleton could be used for errands when a wheelchair or crutches are too hard to use.

Kazerooni's exoskeleton (shown) is powered by two motors at the hips that move the legs forward by pushing buttons on a handheld controller.

Other exoskeleton developers are also building models for medical use. Being able to stand and walk improves a person's physical health. It increases bone density and improves **cardiorespiratory** function while also decreasing pain. All of these elements can help improve a person's mental state. Wearable robots that let people walk upright can improve many lives.

Gene Laureano is an army veteran. His life has changed

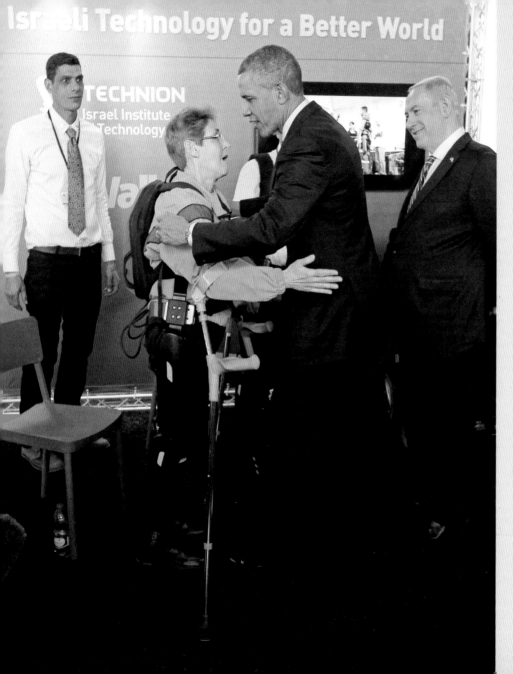

because of robotic exoskeletons. He suffered a spinal injury in 2001 and is paralyzed from the waist down. Using the ReWalk Personal System, he is able to walk on his own. He has used his exoskeleton since 2013. The ReWalk attaches to his legs and is controlled by a communicator watch worn on his wrist. He also wears a backpack that holds a battery pack. The ReWalk has

President Obama hugs a retired soldier at an Israeli event demonstrating the ReWalk Personal System. It was approved for use in the United States in June of 2014.

four movement modes: sitting, standing, walking, and climbing stairs. Each is controlled by the watch.

To walk, Laureano leans slightly forward. A sensor detects his movement that then sends a signal to the robotic exoskeleton. The ReWalk lifts his leg. As Laureano shifts his body back and forth, the sensors signal the robotic legs to take steps. He looks like he is walking with a natural gait.

Strengthening Soldiers

Exoskeletons like the Raytheon Sarcos XOS make soldiers stronger. Exoskeletons let the wearer lift or carry up to 200 pounds (91kg) over and over without tiring. Soldiers wearing one of these robots could carry heavy gear over long distances and

not get tired. They could rescue wounded soldiers in battle with ease. They could use a weapon that normally takes two people. Soldiers would also be able to run farther and not get tired as fast.

Defense technology developer Lockheed Martin is also building an exoskeleton for soldiers. It is called the Human Universal Load Carrier (HULC). It helps reduce stress on a soldier's leg and back muscles. It is a hydraulic system that

Walking Again

In 2012 doctors told Cory Cook of Boston, Massachusetts that he would never walk again. A swimming accident had left him paralyzed from the waist down. By 2015 he was able to take regular walks with his wife and dog. Cook walks with the help of a Re-Walk exoskeleton. He controls the exoskeleton with a Bluetooth watch.

After ten months of using the ReWalk, Cook says that he is not fully independent. When using the ReWalk, he also uses forearm crutches for balance and his wife stays close for support. She also helps him move over uneven ground. Still, Cook says that the ReWalk helps him get stronger. Once he masters walking on even ground, he is eager to try the next challenge: hills.

A paraplegic man demonstrates the ReWalk suit, which enables him to stand, walk, and climb stairs.

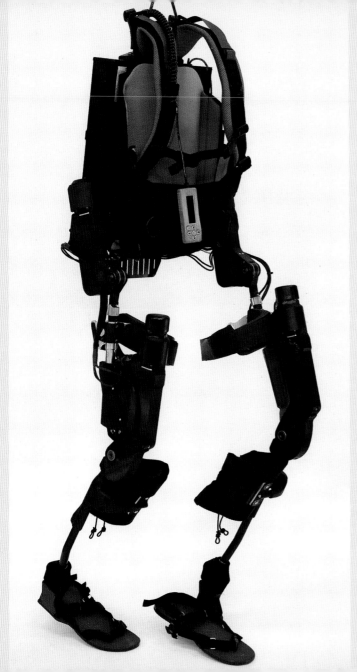

helps a soldier carry pack loads of up to 200 pounds (91kg). With the HULC, a soldier can safely lift heavy loads using the strength of two or more men. At the same time, the HULC's titanium legs let soldiers move freely across different terrains. They can squat, crawl, and

HULC, Human Universal Load Carrier, allows soldiers to carry weights of up to 200 pounds on their backs in all terrains.

Cleaning Up Disaster

In 2011 a tsunami and earthquake hit Japan. They caused the Fukushima Daiichi Nuclear Power Plant to partly melt down. During cleanup efforts, workers used the HAL 5 exoskeleton. The suit let workers wear more protective gear. It also let them work longer shifts and not tire as fast. The HAL 5 is the fifth generation of the first HAL exoskeleton. It is a full-body exoskeleton that weighs 22 pounds (10kg). It senses biosignals on the skin's surface. This lets the exoskeleton mirror the wearer's movement. The HAL 5 lasts for about 90 minutes on a full charge.

lift while wearing it. Most importantly, the battery-powered HULC has enough power to last for an eight-hour march.

Protecting Industrial Workers

Soldiers are not the only ones who could benefit from an exoskeleton. Factory and construction workers often need to use heavy tools and equipment. Their jobs require them to lift heavy loads and carry this weight over a distance. These tasks can take a big physical toll on workers and they may have to take many breaks throughout the day, making them less productive. For companies, lost time costs money. In addition, the stress on workers' bodies can cause injuries and companies

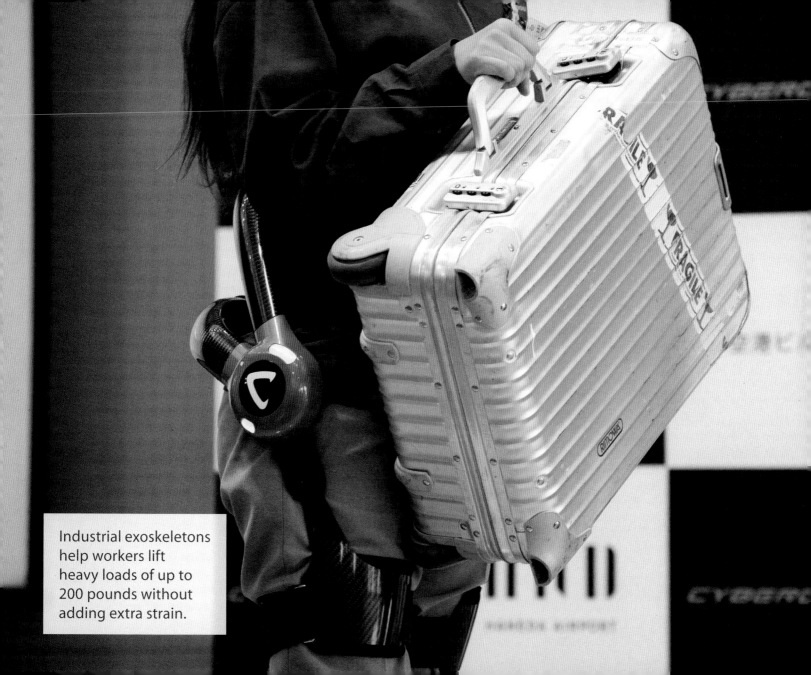

Industrial exoskeletons help workers lift heavy loads of up to 200 pounds without adding extra strain.

end up paying billions of dollars because of injured workers.

Robotic exoskeletons can ease the burden on workers. They can help workers do their jobs without strain. With an exoskeleton, workers may be able to work longer and they may have fewer injuries.

Several companies have already developed devices that help workers. Ekso Works Industrial Exoskeleton lets a worker lift heavy objects and tools as if they weighed nothing at all. The exoskeleton is a metal frame that is strapped over clothing. It has a special arm that can hold tools such as grinders, welders, and other moderately heavy machinery. The suit transfers the weight of whatever the arm is holding down through the suit and into the ground. This greatly reduces stress on the worker's body. A bar on the back holds counterbalance weights to stabilize the worker.

Another exoskeleton for workers is the Body Extender. It is still in the development stage and is being built by the Perceptual Robotics Lab near Pisa, Italy. This exoskeleton would increase a person's strength up to ten times. It would allow workers to lift and handle materials that are too heavy for one person to carry.

It seems clear that robotic exoskeletons may be used in many different ways. From every day workers to helping paralyzed people walk, such suits may transform the way people think about their limitations.

CHAPTER 4

Super Strength in the Future

Where will robotic exoskeletons go in the future? Engineers are improving current models to make them easier to use. Improved wearable robots will be lighter, more flexible, and more accessible. These improvements will allow use of exoskeletons in sports, rehabilitation, and possibly use in outer space.

A Custom Design

Engineers continue to work on smaller, more wearable exoskeletons. Homayoon Kazerooni wants to make simple exoskeletons that people can use at home.

To do this, his team evaluates a person's specific needs and strengths. For example, some people are completely paralyzed. Others can move parts of their body. Also, some people are stronger than others. A patient who has some control of his or her knees does not need a suit that moves the whole leg. Making this change can make the suit up to 10 pounds (4.5kg) lighter.

A paralyzed veteran uses a Kazerooni exoskeleton to help him walk.

In the future, Kazerooni sees a wearable robot that can mix and match features. It would be like getting a prescription for a pair of glasses. Each exoskeleton would be a custom design. A robotic suit with **interchangeable** parts would also be easier and cheaper to make and each person would get exactly what is needed.

Wearing Robots in Outer Space

One day robotic exoskeletons might be used in outer space. NASA engineers are working on an exoskeleton called the X1 Mina Exoskeleton. The X1 is worn over the legs. It has a harness that reaches up the back and around the shoulders. It has four motorized joints at the hips and knees along with six other joints. These let the user step sideways, turn and point, and flex a foot.

NASA thinks that the X1 may one day be used in space to keep astronauts healthy. Because there is no gravity in space, an astronaut's body starts to change on a long mission. Bones lose calcium and the heart weakens because it does not have to work against gravity to

The NASA X1 Mina Exoskeleton is designed to help astronauts work more effectively in space.

pump blood. The astronaut's muscles also get weaker because they do not have to work against gravity. To stay healthy, astronauts exercise for several hours each day.

Scientists are looking at ways for astronauts to use the X1 as an exercise device. In one mode, the X1 gives **resistance** against leg movement. Astronauts could wear it and do resistance exercises. It could keep them healthy without taking up

Lightening Luggage

Lifting heavy luggage can be a backbreaking job. Haneda Airport in Tokyo is giving its workers some extra strength. The airport has partnered with Japanese robotics company Cyberdyne to bring a HAL Lumbar Support robotic exoskeleton to work. When a person moves, the brain sends signals to muscles. Those signals are readable on the skin's surface. HAL suits use skin sensors to read these signals. Then the suit moves the wearer's muscles. It helps a person move just by thinking about it.

The HAL suit that the airport workers will use is small enough for women and elderly workers to wear. Wearing the device, a person who weighs about 110 pounds (50kg) would be able to easily lift luggage up to 45 pounds (20kg). It also gives lower back support when lifting heavy loads.

valuable space or weight on a mission. The X1 can also measure and record the wearer's data. This could be sent to doctors on Earth. It would give them instant information about the astronaut's exercise program and health.

The X1 could also help astronauts on missions outside the spacecraft. Worn with a spacesuit, the X1 could give added strength and force to an astronaut. This could make it easier for astronauts to walk in reduced gravity.

Soft Exosuits

Researchers are also working on ways to make the suits more comfortable. They are working on eliminating the heavy rigid frames and replacing them with fabric. Exosuits made of flexible fabric would be light and efficient. They could be built into the fabric of clothes.

At Harvard University, researcher Conor Walsh is building a flexible exosuit. The suit is designed to improve people's endurance. It is made of nylon, polyester, and spandex. It straps snugly around a user's hips and thighs and connects to boots at the heel. As the user walks, sensors in the boots send a signal to an actuator box that is worn in a backpack or clipped to a belt. A computer uses motors and pulleys to tug on cables that are strapped to the wearer's hips and ankles. This gives a burst of power. When wearing the exosuit, a person uses less energy to walk. Also, the soft exosuit weighs only about 13 pounds (6kg).

Researchers are also working on a robotic fabric that moves and contracts.

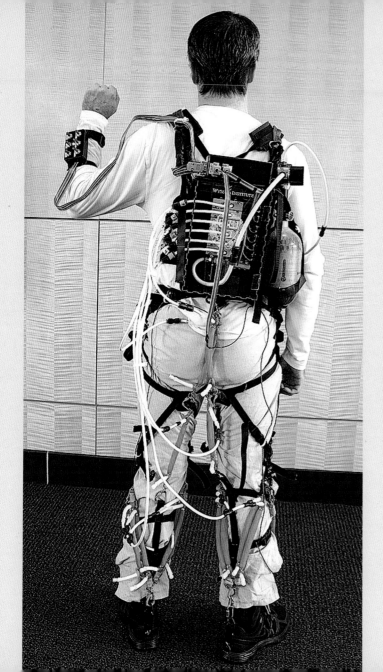

The Harvard Exosuit, developed by Conor Walsh, can improve endurance while wearing the device.

The fabric has sensors and thread-like actuators. One day robotic fabric could be used to make stretchy robotic clothes. People could wear robotic clothes for added strength, endurance, or movement.

Increasing Endurance

Wearable robots may make life easier for millions of people. In particular, soldiers often carry heavy packs for long periods of time. Researchers are working on small exosuit clothing designs for the military. One day soldiers may be able to wear these soft exosuits under their

Honda's Walking Assist Device

Carmaker Honda hopes that its Walking Assist Device will help the elderly and disabled walk. Honda built the device to help people relearn how to walk after a stroke or other injury. It is worn around the hips and thighs. Hip angle sensors take readings of a person's natural gait. A computer controls and activates motors to improve the timing of each leg movement. The device helps lift the wearer's knees when walking. Its motion helps the wearer have a smoother, longer stride. Over time, users will increase strength in their leg muscles and may one day find it easier to walk on their own.

A Honda engineer demonstrates the new model of the company's Walking Assist Device in Tokyo. The device is designed to assist the elderly and disabled people who have weakened leg muscles.

A next-generation atmospheric exosuit diving system.

uniforms. They would be much easier to wear and use than rigid exoskeletons.

Dive Deep

Another form of exoskeletons is the Atmospheric Diving System (ADS). The purpose of this diving system is to maintain water surface pressure when diving deep. The pressure at 1000 ft. (304.8 meters) below sea level is much greater than that of the surface, making it difficult to function and move.

One example of an ADS is the EXO-SUIT produced by Nuytco Research Ltd. in Canada. This hard metal dive suit can take divers to 1000 feet (304.8 meters) below the water's surface without losing dexterity. This allows the diver to perform delicate work. The suit is flexible enough to bend because it has rotary joints developed by Phil Nuytten. Many ADS developments evolve from Dr. Nuytten's work. His original rotary joint patent in 1985 provided the breakthrough that allowed modern ADS systems to evolve as practical subsea equipment.

What to Wear

In only a few years, robotic exoskeletons have leaped from comic books to the real world. As design and technology improve, these wearable robots will become more powerful. They will also be easier to wear. They have the potential to impact and improve many areas of life. Someday wearable robots may be worn by ordinary people around the world.

GLOSSARY

actuators [ACK-tchu-ay-ters]: Types of motors responsible for moving or controlling a mechanism or a system.

amplifier [AMP-luh-fy-er]: A device that takes something small and makes it much larger.

cardiorespiratory [CAR-dee-oh-RES-pir-uh-tor-ee]: The circulatory and respiratory systems of the human body.

decoded [dee-CHOD-ed]: Figured out the meaning of something.

durability [dur-uh-BILL-uh-tee]: The ability to be long lasting and resist wear.

exoskeleton [EKS-oh-skell-uh-tun]: A hard, external covering.

gait rehabilitation [gayt ree-uh-bill-uh-TAY-shun]: A process of helping an injured person relearn how to walk.

hydraulic [hy-DRAW-lick]: A system that is operated or moved by water or other liquids in motion.

interchangeable [in-tur-CHAIN-juh-bull]: The ability to be changed or replaced with another part.

microprocessors [MY-kro-PRAH-sess-urz]: Computer chips that each have the power of a computer's central processing unit (CPU).

prosthetics [prahs-THET-iks]: Artificial body parts.

prototype [PROH-toe-type]: An early version of a product, built to test the design of the product.

resistance [reh-ZIS-tense]: A force that pushes back against something.

sensors [SENS-urz]: Electronic devices that send a signal to a measuring or control instrument.

stationary [STAY-shun-air-ee]: Having a fixed position and not moving.

tendons [TEN-duhnz]: Bands of tough tissue that connect muscles to bones.

terrain [ter-RAYN]: A piece of ground and its physical characteristics.

FOR MORE INFORMATION

Books

Kathy Ceceri, *Robotics: Discover the Science and Technology of the Future*. White River Junction, VT: Nomad, 2012.

Mark Shulman, *Robots*. New York: Time for Kids, 2014. This book goes into detail about many types of robots and includes a chapter on robotic exoskeletons.

Video

The Robotic Exoskeleton, National Geographic Channel. http://channel.nationalgeographic.com /videos/the-robotic-exoskeleton.

Websites

Ekso Bionics (www.eksobionics.com). This is the website of one exoskeleton design company. It shows and explains its designs.

Berkeley Robotics & Human Engineering Laboratory (http://bleex.me.berkeley.edu). This website has detailed information about several different exoskeleton systems currently being developed by Berkeley researchers.

INDEX

Carla Mooney is the author of many books for children and young adults. She lives in Pittsburgh, Pennsylvania with her husband and three children.